CONTENTS

❦ Lake Classic Short Stories ❧

"The universe is made of stories, not atoms."
— Muriel Rukeyser

"The story's about you."
— Horace

Everyone loves a good story. It is hard to think of a friendlier introduction to classic literature. For one thing, short stories are *short*—quick to get into and easy to finish. Of all the literary forms, the short story is the least intimidating and the most approachable.

Great literature is an important part of our human heritage. In the belief that this heritage belongs to everyone, *Lake Classic Short Stories* are adapted for today's readers. Lengthy sentences and paragraphs are shortened. Archaic words are replaced. Modern punctuation and spellings are used. Many of the longer stories are abridged. In all the stories, painstaking care has been taken to preserve the author's unique voice.

Lake Classic Short Stories have something for everyone. The hundreds of stories in the collection cover a broad terrain of themes, story types, and styles. Literary merit was a deciding factor in story selection. But no story was included unless it was as enjoyable as it was instructive. And special priority was given to stories that shine light on the human condition.

Each book in the *Lake Classic Short Stories* is devoted to the work of a single author. Little-known stories of merit are included with famous old favorites. Taken as a whole, the collected authors and stories make up a rich and diverse sampler of the story-teller's art.

Lake Classic Short Stories guarantee a great reading experience. Readers who look for common interests, concerns, and experiences are sure to find them. Readers who bring their own gifts of perception and appreciation to the stories will be doubly rewarded.

❧ Sarah Orne Jewett ❧
(1849–1909)

About the Author

Sarah Orne Jewett lived most of her life in a small village on the seacoast of Maine. Her grandfather was a ship owner, and her father was a doctor. As a child, she often rode with him on his rounds. She never forgot the unique speech patterns she heard in Maine's remote farmhouses and fishing shacks. Years later, her "good ear" for spoken language would distinguish her writing. Her first novel, A *Country Doctor*, is based on memories of her father.

As an adult her closest friendship was with Annie A. Fields, the widow of a Boston publisher. Together, they maintained a "literary salon"—a regular gathering place for writers and their friends to meet and talk. There they entertained such important writers of the day as Henry James and Oliver Wendell Holmes.

The most common theme in Jewett's writing is the contrast between the past and the present, between the country and the town. Her characters are natural. They live at the same pace as the natural world and are affected by such things as the seasons and the weather.

Jewett is known as the best American *regionalist* writer of the 19th century. (A regionalist writer is one whose work is set in a certain region, or area.) Jewett knew her own little corner of the world well, and she wrote about it with a delicate touch. She once said, "The thing that teases the mind over and over for years, and at last gets itself put down rightly on paper— whether little or great, it belongs to Literature." Her story "A White Heron" is generally considered her best.

If you enjoy portraits of ordinary people in a regional setting, you'll find Sarah Orne Jewett's stories quite charming.

A White Heron

Have you ever been tempted to switch loyalties? Only Sylvy has the information that the handsome stranger needs. But helping him would be a kind of betrayal. In this powerful story, a young girl's decision is a true test of character.

"I WOULD GIVE TEN DOLLARS TO ANYBODY WHO COULD
SHOW ME THE HERON'S NEST."

A White Heron

I

The woods were already filled with shadows one June evening, just before eight o'clock. A brief sunset still shone faintly among the trunks of the trees. A little girl was driving home her cow. They were going away from the western light, striking deep into the dark woods. But they were familiar with the path. It didn't matter whether they could see or not.

There was hardly a summer night when the old cow could be found waiting at the pasture fence. In fact, she seemed to love to hide herself away among the bushes. She wore a loud bell, but she had learned that it would not ring if she stood perfectly still. So Sylvia had to hunt for her every evening until she found her.

The cow gave good milk, and plenty of it, so her owners put up with her bad behavior. Besides, Sylvia had plenty of time. Sometimes it was fun to pretend that the cow was playing hide and seek. The child had no playmates, so she enjoyed this little game. Tonight the chase had been long. But Sylvia only laughed when she found Mistress Moolly at the swamp. She urged the animal homeward with a twig of birch leaves. For once, the old cow turned in the right direction and stepped along the road at a good pace. She was quite ready to go home and be milked now.

Sylvia wondered what her grand-mother would say because they were so late. It was a long while since she had left home at 5:30. But everyone knew how hard it was to find this cow. Mrs. Tilley herself had chased the cagey animal on many summer evenings. She would never blame anyone else for taking too long at the task. These days, grandmother was thankful that she had Sylvia to give her so much help.

The good woman guessed that Sylvia sometimes took her time because she was enjoying herself. Since the world was made, there never was such a child for straying about out of doors! Everybody said that the country was a good change for the little girl. After living in a crowded town for eight years, Sylvia loved the country. She felt that she had never been alive at all before she came to live at the farm.

"Afraid of folks," old Mrs. Tilley had thought about Sylvia on that first day. She had chosen Sylvia from her daughter's houseful of children. Then she had brought the girl home with her to help on the farm. "Afraid of folks," she said to herself. "Well, I guess she won't be bothered with too much company up at the old place!" When they had reached the farm house door, the cat had purred and rubbed against them. Sylvia whispered that this was a beautiful place to live. She thought she would never wish to go back home.

Now, the cow and the child followed the shady road—the cow taking slow steps, and the child fast ones. The cow stopped at the brook to drink while Sylvia stood and waited. She let her bare feet cool in the water, while the great twilight moths struck softly against her. Then she waded on through the brook as the cow moved away. Her heart beat fast with pleasure as she listened to the birdsong. Sylvia knew about the stirring in the trees overhead. The treetops were full of little birds and beasts that seemed to be saying goodnight to each other in sleepy twitters. Sylvia herself felt sleepy as she walked along. But it was not too much farther along to the house, and the air was soft and sweet.

She was not often in the woods this late. Now it made her feel that she was a part of all the gray shadows and the moving leaves. Sylvia was thinking how long ago it seemed since she first came to the farm. But it was only a year ago. She wondered if everything went on in the noisy town just the same as when she was there.

Suddenly this little girl in the woods was horror stricken to hear a clear whistle from quite nearby. Not a bird's whistle, but a boy's whistle. Sylvia jumped into the bushes, but she was too late. The enemy had discovered her. Now he called out in a cheerful tone, "Hello, little girl, how far is it to the road?" Trembling, Sylvia answered in a tiny voice, "A good ways."

She did not dare to look directly at the tall young man, who carried a gun over his shoulder. But she came out of hiding and followed the cow. The stranger walked along beside her.

"I have been hunting for some birds," the stranger said kindly. "I have lost my way, and I need a friend very much. Don't be afraid," he added. "Speak up and tell me what your name is. Do you think I can spend the night at your house? I will go out shooting early in the morning."

Sylvia was more alarmed than before. Wouldn't her grandmother be angry with her? But who could have guessed that anything like this would happen? How could it be her fault that the stranger was there? She hung her head like a flower on a broken stem. At last, she managed to answer, "Sylvy."

Old Mrs. Tilley was standing in the doorway when the three figures came into view. The cow gave a loud moo as if to explain.

"Yes, you'd better speak up for yourself, you old troublemaker!" Mrs. Tilley said to the cow. "Where did she hide herself away this time, Sylvy?" Sylvia remained silent. She could see that her grandmother did not understand the situation. She must be mistaking the stranger for one of the farmer lads of the neighborhood.

The young man stood his gun beside the door and dropped a heavy bag of game beside it. He said good evening to Mrs. Tilley and repeated the story he had told Sylvia. He asked if he could spend the night.

"Put me anywhere you like," he said. "I must be off early in the morning. I am very hungry, indeed. You can give me some milk at least, that's plain to see."

"Dear sakes, yes," answered Mrs. Tilley, with great hospitality. "You might find a better supper if you went out on the main road a mile or so. But you're welcome to what we've got. I'll milk right away, and you make yourself at home. Now step round and set a plate for the gentleman, Sylvy!" And Sylvia promptly stepped. She was glad to have something to do, and she was hungry herself.

The stranger was surprised to find such a clean and comfortable house in this New England wilderness. He listened eagerly to the old woman's talk. He watched Sylvia's pale face and shining gray eyes with growing interest. Later, he insisted that this was the best supper he had eaten for a month.

Afterward, the new-made friends sat on the doorstep together and watched the moon come up.

Soon it would be berry time, Sylvia's grandmother said, and Sylvia was a great help at picking. The cow was a good milker, though a bothersome thing to keep track of. The grandmother talked on and on, adding that four of her children had died. Sylvia's mother and a son in California were all the children she had left.

"Dan, my boy, was a great hunter," she said sadly. "We had all the squirrels and birds we needed while he was at home. But he loves to travel—and he isn't much at writing letters. I don't blame him, though. I'd have been off to see the world myself if I could have.

"Sylvia here takes after him," the grandmother continued. "There ain't a foot of ground she don't know her way over. The wild animals think she's one of them. She tames squirrels to eat right out of her hands, and all sorts of birds."

The stranger's ears pricked up.

"So Sylvy knows all about birds, does she?" he said, smiling. "I am making a collection of birds myself. I have been at it ever since I was a boy. There are two or three very rare ones I have been hunting for five years. I mean to have them if they can be found."

"Do you put them in cages?" asked Mrs. Tilley.

"Oh, no, I stuff them—dozens and dozens of them," said the bird collector. "I shot or snared every one of them myself. On Saturday, I caught a glimpse of a white heron just three miles from here. I followed it in this direction. They have never been found in this part of the country at all." Hoping to discover that the rare bird was one of her friends, he turned to Sylvia.

But Sylvia was watching a toad in the footpath.

"You would know the heron if you saw it," the stranger continued eagerly. "It's a strange, tall, white bird with soft feathers and long thin legs. Its nest would probably be found up in the top of a high tree."

Sylvia's heart gave a wild beat. She knew that strange white bird. She had once stolen softly near it in some bright green swamp grass. That was away over at the other side of the woods. There was an open place there, where tall, nodding rushes grew. Her grandmother had warned her about the mud around the rushes. She said that Sylvy might sink in that soft black and never be heard of again. Not far beyond that place was a salt marsh, and beyond that was the sea. Sylvia had often wondered and dreamed about the sea, but she had never seen it. Sometimes she had heard it above the noise of the woods on stormy nights.

"I can't think of anything I should like more than to find that heron's nest," the handsome stranger was saying. "I would give ten dollars to anybody who could show it to me," he added desperately. "I mean to spend my whole vacation hunting for it, if need be."

Mrs. Tilley gave amazed attention to all this, but Sylvia still watched the toad. At another time, she would have realized that the toad wanted to get to its hole under the doorstep. But tonight, she was wondering how many treasures ten dollars might buy.

The next day the young hunter explored the woods, and Sylvia kept him company. He told her many things about the birds. He talked on and on about where they lived and what they did with themselves. And he gave her a jackknife, which was a great treasure. All day long he did not once make her troubled or afraid—except when he shot some unsuspecting, singing creature. Sylvia would have liked the young man much better without his gun. She could not understand why he killed the very birds he seemed to like so much.

At last evening began to fall, and they drove the cow home together. Soon they came to the place where the stranger's whistle had frightened her only the night before. As they passed, Sylvia smiled.

II

A great pine tree stood, half a mile from home, at the far edge of the woods. It towered above all the other trees and was used as a landmark from miles and miles away. Sylvia knew it well. She had always believed that whoever climbed to the top of that tree could see the ocean. Often, the little girl had laid her hand on the trunk and looked up with wonder into the dark branches. Now she thought of the tree with a new excitement. If someone climbed it at break of day, could not that person see all of the world? Wouldn't it be easy, then, to find the white heron and its hidden nest?

What a great adventure! What glory later when she could tell the secret! The thought was almost too real and too great for her to bear!

All night the door of the little house stood open. The young hunter and the grandmother were sound asleep. But Sylvia's great plan kept her wide awake and watching. At last, just before morning came, she stole out of the house and followed the path through the woods.

There was the huge tree, still asleep in the paling moonlight. Small and hopeful, Sylvia began bravely to climb. First she had to climb the white oak that grew beside the pine. Her bare feet and fingers pinched and held like bird's claws. The great trunk reached up, up, almost to the sky itself. She was almost lost among the dark branches and the green leaves, heavy and wet with dew. A bird fluttered off its nest, and a red squirrel ran to and fro, scolding. But Sylvia felt her way easily. She had often climbed there. She knew where one of the oak's high branches touched the pine trunk.

At last she crept out along the swaying oak limb. Then she took the daring step across into the old pine tree. The way was harder than she thought. Sharp dry twigs caught and scratched her. Her thin little fingers grew stiff and clumsy as she went round and round the tree's great trunk. She climbed higher and higher upward. Below, the sparrows and robins were beginning to wake and twitter to the dawn. It seemed much lighter so high up in the pine tree. The child knew that she must hurry.

The tree seemed to get longer and longer as she went up. With every gain she made, the tree reached farther and farther upward.

Sylvia's face looked like a pale star, if anyone had seen it from the ground. At last she stood trembling and tired high in the treetop. Yes, there was the sea with the dawning sun making a golden dazzle over it. Two hawks flew by heading east. How low they looked from that height! Their gray feathers were as soft as moths. They seemed so close to the tree that Sylvia felt as if she, too, could go flying away among the clouds.

The birds sang louder and louder as the sun came up. Sylvia could see the white sails of ships out at sea. Where was the white heron's nest in the sea of green branches? Now look down again, Sylvia, where the green marsh lies among the birches and hemlocks. There—where you saw the white heron once, you will see him again.

Look! Look! A white spot of him comes up from the dead hemlock and grows larger. It rises, and comes close at last. It flies by the tall pine with steady sweep of wing and outstretched slender neck and crested head. And wait! Wait! Do not move a foot or a finger, little girl. Do you see? The heron has perched on a pine branch not far beyond yours. He cries back to his mate on the nest. Now he plumes his feathers for the new day!

The child knows his secret now. She has seen the wild, light, slender bird floating through the air. She knows that his home is in the dead hemlock tree. Well satisfied, Sylvia makes her way down again. She dares not look far below the branch she's on. Sometimes she is ready to cry because her fingers ache and her torn feet slip. Over and over again she wonders what the stranger would say to her if he knew. What would he think when she told him how to find his way straight to the heron's nest?

"Sylvy, Sylvy!" called the busy old grandmother. Again and again she called, but nobody answered. The small bed was empty, and Sylvia had disappeared.

The guest awoke and hurried to dress. He had noticed the way the shy little girl looked once or twice yesterday. That knowing look had given him a clue. He was sure that she had at least seen the white heron. Now she must really be persuaded to tell.

Here she comes now, paler than ever, and her dress is torn and tattered. The grandmother and the hunter stand in the door together and question her. The splendid moment has come. It is time to speak of the dead hemlock tree by the green marsh.

But Sylvia does not speak after all. The young man's kind eyes look straight into her own. He can make them rich with money. He has promised it, and they are poor. To Sylvia, he is well worth making happy, and now he waits to hear the story she can tell.

No, she must keep silence! What is it that suddenly forbids her to speak? She has spent nine years growing. Now the great world has put a hand out to her for the first time. Must she push that hand aside for a bird's sake? The murmur of the pine's green branches is in her ears. She remembers how the white heron came flying through the golden air. She remembers how they watched the sea and the morning together. Sylvia cannot speak. She cannot tell the heron's secret and give its life away.

The disappointed guest went away later in the day. Many a night after that, Sylvia heard the echo of his whistle as she came home with the wandering cow. Slowly she forgot her sorrow at the sharp sound of his gun. She forgot even the pitiful sight of the tiny thrushes and sparrows, dropping silent to the ground.

She no longer remembered how their songs were hushed and their feathers made wet with blood.

Were the birds better friends than their hunter might have been? Who can tell? Whatever treasures were lost to her, woodlands and summer time remember: Bring your gifts and graces and tell your secrets to this lonely country child!

❧

The Hiltons' Holiday

Few children today would be thrilled about taking an uncomfortable trip to a small town. But the hard-working farm families of 100 years ago rarely left home. This is a story about simple pleasures in a bygone time. Of all the author's stories, she said that this was her favorite.

THE OUTING WAS SUCH A RARE EVENT THAT THE LITTLE
GIRLS WERE SPEECHLESS.

The Hiltons' Holiday

I

A bright, full moon rose in the clear sky, while the sunset was still shining faintly in the west. Dark woods stood all about the old Hilton farmhouse. Just down the hill lay the fields that John Hilton and his father had cleared and farmed. To these small fields the two men had given all the work and love of their honest lives.

John Hilton was sitting on the front doorstep of his house. His peaceful face showed him to be a man at home with the brown earth, instead of the noisy town. It was late in the long spring evening. John had just come up from the lower field. Cheerful as a boy, he was proud of having finished planting his potatoes.

"I had to do the last row mostly by feeling my way along," he said to his wife. "But I'm glad I went back after supper and got it done."

"Ain't no use for you to work yourself all to pieces, John," said the woman. "I declare, sometimes it seems harder than ever that we lost our boy. He'd be 14 years old this fall. He'd be working right alongside of you now."

"I do miss little John," said the father sadly. "But I expect that what happened was for the best. Maybe someday we'll know the reason. I feel plenty able to work the farm alone. But I was thinking, by myself today, what grand company the boy would have been. You know, small as he was, how I could trust him. I was remembering how he'd beg to go with me wherever I was going. I used to tell him he was always right in my tracks. Poor little John, young as he was, he had a lot of judgment. He'd have made a fine man."

The mother sighed sadly and looked down at her hands.

"But then there's the little girls," John went on. "They're a lot of help and they're company, too," he said. He smiled broadly now, as if it were wrong to dwell upon sorrow and loss. "Katy—she's 'most as good as a boy, except that she ain't very tough. But she's a real little farmer. She's helped me a lot this spring. And you've got Susan Ellen. Already she's a good little housekeeper. We're better off than most folks—each of us having a workmate."

"That's so, John," Mrs. Hilton agreed. She began to rock in her chair. It was always a good sign when she rocked.

"Where are the little girls so late?" asked their father. "It's past eight o'clock. I don't know when we've sat up so late, but it's like a summer evening. Where did they go?"

"Only over to Becker's folks," answered the mother. "I don't see, myself, what keeps them so late. After supper they begged till I let them go. They're all excited about the new teacher. She asked them to come over. They say she's really good with arithmetic. She's going to give Katy some clothes for her doll. But I told Katy she ought to be ashamed to want dolls' clothes, big as she's getting to be. I don't know, though—she's only nine."

"Let her enjoy herself," said the kind-hearted man. "Those things will help her to get to know her teacher. Katy's shy with new folks. Susan Ellen is more like the business kind. Katy's shy-feeling and wishful."

"Well, that's true," agreed the mother. "Ain't it odd how well you understand that one—and I do Susan Ellen? It was that way from the beginning. I doubt sometimes that our Katy will ever get married. She gets along fine just with herself, but not Susan Ellen. She's always wanting company. The boys are running after her already. She'll take her pick when the time comes. I expect to see Susan Ellen well married—she feels grown up now. But Katy just wants to be roaming around outdoors. I do believe she'd stand and watch a bird all afternoon."

"Could be she'll grow up to be a teacher," John Hilton thought aloud. "She takes to her books more than the other one. I would like one of them to be a teacher, like my mother. Those girls are as good as anybody's got."

"So they are," said the mother, rocking. The night breeze stirred in the great woods, and the sound of a brook grew louder. Now and then the chirp of a bird sang out. The moon shone upon the low-roofed house until its small window-panes gleamed like silver. The bright moonlight lit up even the blooming lilac bush that grew by the kitchen door. Frogs sang in the lowlands.

"Are you sound asleep, John?" asked the wife.

"Maybe I was—almost," said the tired man. "It's the bright night that makes my eyes feel heavy. Maybe I'd better step along and meet the little girls."

"I wouldn't just yet. They'll get home all right. Let's wait a few minutes," said Mrs. Hilton.

"I've been thinking all day I'd like to give the children some kind of a treat," said the father. He was wide awake now. "I hurried up my work because I had it so in mind. They don't have the chances some children do. I want them to know the world, and not be stuck here on the farm like a couple of bushes."

"They're a lot better off than some who are full of big ideas," protested the mother.

"True," answered the farmer, "but they're good, bright children. They're starting to notice the world around them. I want them to have all that we can give them. I want them to see how other folks do things."

"Well, so do I," she said. The rocking chair stopped. "But as long as they're contented—"

"Contentment ain't all there is in the world. Hopper toads may be contented. I don't think contentment's everything for a child. I think ambition means something, too."

"Now you've got some kind of plot in mind," Mrs. Hilton said. Her rocking chair began to move again. "Why can't you say it right out?"

"It ain't nothing special," answered the good man. He was always surprised when his wife seemed to read his mind. "Well there, you do find things out! I only thought I'd take them off tomorrow if it was a good day. I've been promising for a long while to take them to Topham Corners. They haven't been there since they were very small."

"I believe you want a good time for yourself," she said. "You ain't never got over being a boy!" Mrs. Hilton seemed much amused. "There, go if you want to— and take them. They've got their summer hats and new dresses. I don't know that anything stands in the way. Too bad there ain't a circus or anything to go to. But why don't you wait and let the girls pick some strawberries or some nice roseberries? Then they could take them and sell them in the stores."

John Hilton thought a while. "I would like to get me some good yellow-turnip seed. And I'm going to get me a good hoe. Mine's getting worn out. I can't seem to fix it right."

"Those are excuses," said Mrs. Hilton, in a friendly manner. "But you cover up that hoe with something, if you get it. That Ira Speed's a jealous man. He'll remember for 20 years if you go and buy a new hoe from anybody but him."

"I've always thought it was a free country," said John Hilton. "But I don't want to make Ira mad. He does a lot for us. It's hard for him to spare a cent, but he's as honest as daylight."

At this moment there was a sudden sound of young voices. A pair of small figures came out from the woods into the moonlight. As if royalty had arrived, the old rooster crowed loudly from his perch in the shed. The little girls came up to the house, hand in hand. A small dog danced about them as they walked along.

"Wasn't it dark coming through the woods this time of night?" asked the mother. There was a hint of scolding in her voice.

"I don't like to have you gone so late. Mother and I have been worried about you," said their father. "And you've kept Miss Becker's folks up, I expect. I don't want to have it said that my little girls ain't got good manners."

"The teacher had a party," chirped Susan Ellen, the older of the two children. "She invited the Grover boys and Mary and Sarah Speed. And Miss Becker was real pleasant to us! She passed round some cake and gave us sap sugar on one of her best plates. We played games and sang, too. Miss Becker thought we did real well. I can pick out most of a tune on the organ. Teacher says she'll give me lessons."

"Oh, tell us about it!" exclaimed John Hilton.

"Yes, and we took sides spelling. Katy was the best speller of everyone there."

Katy had not spoken. She seated herself close to her father on the doorstep. He put his arm around her shoulders and drew her close to his side.

"And ain't you got nothing to tell, daughter?" he asked her, looking down fondly. As her answer, Katy gave only a pleased little sigh.

Then a gleam came into her eye. "Tell them what's going to happen the last day of school! Tell about our trimming the schoolhouse," she said to her sister. Susan Ellen told the whole program, with high excitement.

"It will be a fine time," said the mother. "I don't see why folks want to go running off to strange places. Not when such things as this are happening right around them." But the children did not notice her mysterious air. "Come, you girls! Get yourselves right to bed now!"

They all went into the dark, warm house. The moon shone brightly all night.

No breath of wind shook the lilac flowers until dawn.

II

The Hiltons always awoke early, and so did their neighbors. These were the crows and song sparrows and robins, the light-footed foxes and squirrels in the woods. When John Hilton woke up, it was just before five o'clock. This was an hour later than usual—because he had sat up so late the night before.

Now he opened the door and came out into the yard. He marched across it in a great hurry. It was hard for him to believe that he was taking a whole day for pleasure. But the weather was fair, and his wife had smiled upon the great project. He and the children were going to Topham! Mrs. Hilton woke up the girls and told them the good news.

In a few minutes they came frisking out to talk to their father. They found that the cattle were already fed, and their father was milking. The only unusual sign was the wagon pulled out into the yard. Both seats were put in, as if it were Sunday. But Mr. Hilton still wore his everyday clothes. For a minute, Susan Ellen felt a pang of disappointment.

"Ain't we going, Father?" she asked. But he nodded and smiled at her, even though the cow kept whisking its tail across his face. He held his head down and spoke cheerfully, in spite of this insult.

"Yes, sister, we're going," he said "and we're going to have a great time, too." Susan Ellen thought he spoke like a boy at that moment, and she felt delighted. "You go and help Mother with breakfast. We want to get off as quick as we can. And you and your sister see if you can't get your mother to go with us."

"She said you couldn't pay her to go," answered Susan Ellen. "She says it's going to be hot. And she wants to go over and see Auntie Tamsen Brooks this afternoon."

An hour later the wagon was ready, and the great expedition set forth. The little dog barked with wild excitement. The girls, dressed alike in their Sunday hats of straw with blue ribbons, sat on the back seat. Their little plaid shawls were pinned neatly about their small shoulders. They wore gray gloves and sat very straight. Susan Ellen was half a head the taller, but from behind, they looked much alike. As for their father, he was in his Sunday best. He wore a plain black coat and a winter hat of black felt. The hat was hot-looking for that warm day. He had in mind to buy a new straw hat at Topham. With the turnip seed and the hoe, this made three important reasons for going.

"Remember to take off your shawls when you get there. Carry them over your arms," said the mother. She clucked like an excited hen to her chicks. "Don't get spots on you when you eat dinner. And don't point at folks and stare as you ride by—or they'll know that you come from the country. And John, you call by

Cousin Adeline Marlow's and see how they all are. And don't come home all worn out. And John, don't you go buying me any presents. I ain't a child, and you ain't got no money to waste. I expect you'll go and buy yourself some kind of foolish boy's hat. Do make sure it's good straw. And you mind, John—"

"Yes, yes, yes, hold on!" cried John impatiently. Then he smiled at her flushed face. "I wish you were going, too," he said. Then the old horse started the careful, long descent of the hill. The young dog, tied to the lilac bush, jumped and barked as the little girls called their good-bys again and again. Their father turned many times to look back and wave his hand. As for their mother, she stood alone and watched them out of sight.

"They're nothing but a pack of children together," she cried aloud. Then she felt lonelier than she expected. She even patted the miserable little dog as she went into the house.

The outing was such a rare event that both little girls were speechless. At first it seemed like going to church in new clothes. They hardly knew how to behave at the beginning of a whole day of pleasure. As they went along the road, they nodded at people they knew. Once or twice they stopped in front of a farmhouse. They waited as patiently as they could while their father talked with someone about the crops and the weather. Each small homestead shared the beauty of early summer. There was an early peony or late lilac in almost every dooryard.

It was about 17 miles to Topham. After a while they seemed very far from home. They had left the hills behind and descended to level country. There were wider fields and fewer trees here. The houses here were all painted, and the roads were smoother and wider. It had been so pleasant driving along that Katy now dreaded going into the strange town. But Susan Ellen kept asking if they were almost there.

The girls counted the steeples of four churches as they entered the town. Their father showed them the old Topham Academy, where their grandmother had gone to school. He told them that perhaps someday they would go there too. Katy's heart gave a great leap to think of such a wondrous thing.

Soon the children found themselves among the crowded village houses. Their father turned to look at his daughters closely.

"Now sit up straight and look pretty," he whispered to them. "I want folks to think well of you."

"I guess we're as good as they are," said Susan Ellen.

But Katy tried to sit up straighter. She folded her hands in her lap and wished with all her heart to be pleasing for her father's sake.

"Now we're coming to a grand house that I want you to see. You'll never forget it," said John Hilton. "It's where Judge Masterson lives. He's a great lawyer. And his place is the most handsome house in the county, everybody says."

"Do you know the Judge, Father?" asked Susan Ellen.

"I do," answered John Hilton proudly. "He and my mother went to school together. Everybody said they were the two best students of their time. The Judge called to see her once, when I was a boy. And another time, when I saw him in the town, he asked about your grandmother. He spoke most beautifully of her. He told me how fondly he remembered their young days together."

"I'd like to hear about that," said Katy.

"I'm afraid things were pretty hard for your grandmother on the farm. People say she lived longer up in the hills than she could anywhere. But she never had her health. I was just a boy when she died. Afterward Father and I lived alone—till your mother came. It was lonesome, I tell you. Father was sad over losing his wife. Her long sickness killed something inside of him. All day we'd work on the land and he'd never say a word. I suppose being so lonesome early in life made its mark on me, too. That must be what makes me so pleased to have some nice girls growing up around me now."

The tone in her father's voice drew Katy's heart to him. She understood his feelings. But Susan Ellen was less interested—they had often heard this story before. To the one child, the story was always new and to the other always old. Susan Ellen thought it somewhat tiresome to hear about her grandmother. After all, she was dead, and hardly worth talking about.

"There's Judge Masterson's place," said their father, as they turned a corner. They saw a beautiful old white house standing behind green trees and lawns. The children had never imagined anything so stately and fine. Even Susan Ellen exclaimed with pleasure. Then, at that moment, they saw an old gentleman walking slowly down the path toward the gate.

"There he is now," whispered John Hilton in an excited voice. "That's Judge

Masterson." He reined in the horse. "He must be going downtown to his office. We can wait right here and see him. I can't expect him to remember me. It's been too many years."

The Judge stopped at his gate. He glanced up the street at the country wagon. The Judge smiled as he came out to the sidewalk and turned their way. Then he suddenly lifted his hat and came directly toward them.

"Good morning, Mr. Hilton," he said. "I am very glad to see you, sir." The surprised Mr. Hilton took off his hat and bent forward to shake hands.

"These are your daughters, I am sure," said the old gentleman kindly. He took Susan Ellen's hand. Then he looked at Katy and his face lit up. "How she looks like your mother!" he exclaimed. "I am glad to see this dear child. You must come with your father to see me, my dear," he added, still looking at her. "Bring both the little girls, of course. Let them run about the old garden. The cherries are just getting ripe. Perhaps you will have time to stop this afternoon as you go home?"

"Yes, and it would be a great pleasure if you would come and see us some time. You may be driving our way, sir," said John Hilton.

"Not very often any more," answered the old judge. "But I thank you for the kind invitation. I would like to see the fine view from your hill again. Let me know if I can do anything for you while you are in town. Good-by, my little friends!"

Then they parted. The shy Katy lifted her face to kiss him. She could not have said why, except that she felt drawn to something in the old judge's worn face.

"Now you have met one of the finest gentlemen in the county," said their father proudly.

In the business street of Topham, a great many country wagons like the Hiltons' were fastened to hitching posts. To the girls, the busy scene seemed very noisy and exciting.

"Now I've got to do my errands," said their father. "We can let the horse rest and feed. After that, we'll go and buy me a straw hat. Then we'll walk along the street. You can look in the windows and see the handsome things—as your mother likes to do. What was it Mother told you about your shawls?"

"To take them off and carry them over our arms," piped up Susan Ellen. But the shawls soon were forgotten in all the excitement. The children stood outside while their father went inside a shop. They tried to examine the styles of the Topham bonnets, as their mother had told them. But everything was too exciting and confusing. They could sort nothing out. When Mr. Hilton came out with a new straw hat in his hand, Katy whispered to him. She said that she wished he would buy a shiny one like Judge Masterson's. But her father only smiled and shook his head. He said that they were plain folks and that a straw hat was good enough for him.

It was a wonderful day. The girls quickly grew used to seeing so many people pass. The village was full of morning activity. And Susan Ellen gained a new respect for her father. Even in Topham many people knew him and greeted him by name.

"Now I want to buy something pretty for your mother," said Mr. Hilton, as they went up the street. "By now the horse will be rested, and we can jog along home pretty soon. But first I'm going to take you round by the academy. Can you think of something that you mother would want?"

"She was talking about needing a new pepper box. The top of the old one won't stay on," suggested Susan Ellen. "Can't we have some candy, Father?"

"Yes, ma'am," said John Hilton, smiling and swinging her hand to and fro. "I would like some myself. What's all this?" They were passing by the doorway of a photographer. "I do declare!" he exclaimed. "I'm going to have our pictures taken. Your mother would just love that."

This was, without a doubt, the greatest excitement of the day—except for meeting up with the Judge. In the photographer's studio, they sat in a row, with the father in the middle. Both Susan Ellen and Katy looked their brightest and best. The joy of the holiday was mirrored in the little picture.

Just at nightfall the Hiltons reached home again, tired out but happy. It was a cool evening, and the sky was growing cloudy. Somehow the children looked different. It seemed to their mother as if they had grown older and taller since they went away that morning. Now they seemed to belong to the town as much as to the country. Mrs. Hilton's day had been silent and lonely without them. She had their supper ready and had been watching for them since five o'clock. The children could hardly wait to show her the picture, and their mother was very pleased.

"There, why are you still wearing your shawls?" she exclaimed. "Did you wear them all day long? I wanted folks to see how pretty your new dresses are, if I did make them myself."

"And here's the pepper box!" cried Katy.

"That really is beautiful," said Mrs. Hilton, after a long look. "I never expected a shiny one with flowers, but I can get us another for every day. That's a proper hat—as good as you could have gotten, John. Where's your new hoe?"

"I declare, I forgot all about it," said the leader of the great excursion. "That and my yellow-turnip seed, too. But I can get a hoe just as well at Ira Speed's."

His wife could not help laughing. "You and the girls have had a fine time, I see. I guess we were right about having them see something more of the world."

"Yes," answered John Hilton. "We did have a beautiful day. I didn't expect so much. The girls looked just as nice as anybody—so modest and pretty. I guess they won't ever forget this day they had with Father."

The frogs were piping in the meadows. In the woods, a little owl began to hoot. A lamp was lighted in the house. The happy children were talking together, and supper was waiting. For a moment the father and mother stood outside and looked down over the fields. Then they went in. The great day was over, and they shut the door.

Fame's Little Day

Have you ever heard of a
"big fish in a little pond"?
Mr. Abel Pinkham is just
that in his small hometown
in Vermont. Now he and
his wife are having a
holiday in New York City.
Why has their visit been
written up in all the big city
newspapers? Is he more
important than he thought?
Or is a reporter having a
little fun with him?

"JUST YOU LOOK HERE! I'D LIKE TO KNOW HOW THEY
FOUND OUT ABOUT OUR COMING!"

Fame's Little Day

I

Nobody ever knew, except himself, what made the foolish young newspaper reporter do what he did. It was pure chance that the reporter happened to be in the small hotel that day. A Mr. Abel Pinkham from Vermont had just arrived there for a stay with his wife. The reporter observed Mr. Pinkham with deep interest. He listened to his colorful country talk and asked the hotel clerk a few questions. Then he went away and made up a little story for the morning newspapers.

He must have had a heart full of fun, this young reporter. Something about Mr. Pinkham's pleasant country ways must have impressed him.

Perhaps that's why there was a special flavor to what he wrote. Perhaps that explains why his fellow writers noticed the little story. But for whatever reason, they copied it, added to it, and kept it moving. Nobody knows what starts such a thing in newspaper reporting—or keeps it alive after it has started.

But on a certain Thursday morning, the little story appeared in all the New York newspapers. It made known to the world that—among other important visitors—Abel Pinkham, Esquire, of Wetherford, Vermont, had arrived in New York. He had come, the story went, to take care of important matters connected with Vermont's maple-sugar industry. The story said that Mr. Pinkham had expected to keep his visit unannounced. But the reporter was certain that the news would be of great interest to all the city's business leaders.

Here and there, the newspaper reporter's friends had added a line or two. There was news about the length of Mr. Pinkham's stay, and the floor on which he was staying at the Ethan Allen Hotel. And there were plenty of other details. The story was boring to most readers, of course. It was thrown out of the next day's papers. Having had their fun, all the young reporters then went on to write of other things.

Mr. and Mrs. Pinkham had left home with many misgivings. It is true that they had talked about taking this journey all winter. But, once the spring arrived, they would have grabbed at any excuse to stay at home in Vermont. Mrs. Abel Pinkham had never seen New York. Her husband himself had not been to the city for many years.

In fact, Mr. Pinkham's memories of his first visit were not pleasant. He had been cruelly tricked by many New Yorkers. They had taken advantage of his country background. For example, he had paid a lot of money for a worthless fake gold watch. And this was not the only way in which he had been duped by city slickers. Ever since, he had suffered at the thought of their dishonest ways. But he was now a man of 60. He was well-to-do, and well respected in his home town. His children were all well married and settled in homes of their own.

A grown-up grandson had been left in charge of things at home. After all, the maple sugar had already been made and shipped. And it was still too early to start spring work on the land. So Mr. Pinkham could leave home without worrying about his business.

Now here he was in New York, feeling very much a stranger to city ways. He wanted very much to look good in his wife's eyes. If not for that, Mr. Pinkham could happily have taken the next train back to Vermont.

He could not let his wife discover that the noise and confusion of Broadway made him nervous. He told himself that Broadway was no more frightening than his own woods in snow-time! He was as good as anybody, he said to himself—and she was better! They owed nobody a cent, and they had come on purpose to see the city of New York.

On that first morning, they were sitting at the breakfast table in the Ethan Allen Hotel. Mrs. Pinkham looked a little pale. Nearly all night she had been kept awake by the noise. She had not enjoyed at all the evening before, sitting in the hotel's hot and airless parlor. Two young women were her only companions in the parlor. Both of them seemed loud and unpleasant to her. From the window, the activity she saw down on the streets appeared harsh and rude.

Mr. Pinkham was not as uncomfortable in the hotel smoking-room as his wife was in the parlor. He felt much more at home than she did. For one thing, he was more used to meeting strangers than she was. He had quickly found two or three companions who had seen more of New York life than he had.

It was here, in fact, that the young reporter had found him. The reporter was charmed by Mr. Pinkham's hearty, country-fed appearance. He admired Mr. Pinkham's best country clothes, and the way he brushed his hair. But most of all the young man loved the way that Mr. Pinkham loudly voiced the beliefs of his honest heart.

The Pinkhams were feeling very unhappy at breakfast that morning. They missed their feather bed at home. They were troubled by the roar and noise of the streets. The waiter was slow in serving them. Mrs. Pinkham, who was a superb cook herself, did not think much of the hotel's food. She was a woman of imagination. Now that she was really here, it pained her to find that the New York of her dreams did not seem to exist. Where was the great metropolis of dignity and distinction? Where was the refinement and elegance? These dirty streets, these rude people, were the end of a great illusion. Mr. and Mrs. Pinkham did not like to meet each other's eyes. He began to huff and puff, and Mrs. Pinkham's face grew full of dismay.

"My gracious me, Mary Ann! I am glad I happened to get the *Tribune* this morning," said Mr. Pinkham, with sudden excitement. "Just you look here! I'd like to know how they found out about our coming!" He handed the paper to his wife across the table. "There—there it is, right by my thumb," he insisted. "Can't you see it?" He was smiling like a boy as she finally peered through her eyeglasses at the important paragraph.

"I guess they think something of us— even if you don't think much of them!" continued Mr. Pinkham, grandly. "Oh, they know how to keep track of folks who are somebody back home! Draper and Fitch knew that we were coming this week. You know I sent word myself that I was coming to do business with them. I suppose they sent newspaper reporters around to the hotels. But I wouldn't have thought they had enough time for that. Anyway, they thought it was worth while to put us in the paper!"

Mrs. Pinkham didn't bother to make a mystery of the unexpected attention. "I want to cut it out. Let's send it right up home to daughter Sarah," she said, beaming with pride. She looked at their printed names as if they were dazzling photographs. "I think it's a might too strong to say we are *notables*," she said. "But there! It's their business to dress up things. And they *do* have to print something every day. I guess I will go up and put on my best dress," she added. "This one's kind of dusty. It's the same one I rode down in."

"Let me see that paper again," said Mr. Pinkham. "I didn't half read it, I was so surprised. Well, Mary Ann, you didn't expect to get into the papers when you came away, did you? *'Abel Pinkham, Esquire, of Wetherford, Vermont.'* It looks fine, don't it? But you could have knocked me over with a feather when I first caught sight of them words."

"I guess I *will* put on my other dress," Mrs. Pinkham said to herself. Then she rose, with quite a different air from that with which she had sat down to her morning meal. "This one looks a little out of style, as Sarah said. But when I got up this morning, I was so homesick it didn't seem to make any difference. I expect that rude maid last night took us to be nobodies. I'd like to leave the paper around where she would see it."

"Don't take any notice of her," said Abel, in a dignified tone. "If she can't be polite, we'll go somewhere else. I wish I'd done what we talked of at first. We should have gone to the Astor House. But that young man on the train told me it was too far from all the things we should see. When I was here last, the Astor House was the best hotel in town. But I expected to find things changed. I want you to have the best there is," he said, smiling at his wife as if they were on their honeymoon. "Come on, let's be stirring. It's long past eight o'clock!" And he led her to the door, with his newspaper in hand.

II

Later that day Mr. and Mrs. Pinkham strolled up Broadway. They were walking tall and feeling as if every eye was upon them. Just that morning Abel Pinkham had settled with his business partners for the spring orders of maple sugar. Now a large sum of money was stowed away in his breast pocket.

One of the partners, a man named Fitch, had been a Wetherford boy. He remembered that there never was any sugar as delicious as that from the trees on the old Pinkham farm. Fitch had made a lot of money for himself on this sugar and was ready to pay Mr. Abel Pinkham in cash. In addition, he gave Mr. Pinkham a handsome order for next season. The man was immensely polite and kind to his old friends. He begged them to come out and stay with his family at their home in New Jersey.

"No, no, Fitch," said Mr. Pinkham to his kind friend. "My wife has come to see the *city*—and our time is short. Your folks

will be up this summer, won't they? We'll
wait and visit then."

"You must take Mrs. Pinkham to
Central Park," said Fitch. "I wish I had
time to show you around myself. I
suppose you've been seeing some things
already, haven't you? I noticed your
arrival in the *Herald*."

"The *Tribune* it was," Mr. Pinkham
said. He blushed through a smile and
looked around at his wife.

"Oh, no. I never read the *Tribune*,"
said Mr. Fitch. "There was quite a long
notice in *my* paper. They must have put
you and Mrs. Pinkham into the *Herald*,
too." And so the friends parted, laughing.
"I am much pleased to have a call from
such distinguished visitors," said Mr.
Fitch. In reply, Mr. Pinkham waved his
hand grandly.

"Let's get the *Herald*, then," he said to
his wife, as they started up the street.
"We can go and sit over in that little
square we passed as we came along. We'll
rest a bit and talk about what to do this
afternoon. I'm all tired out. I wanted to

sit still for a while, but he wanted us to see his store. Done very well, Joe Fitch has. But it ain't a business *I* would like."

There was a grand look about Mr. Pinkham of Wetherford. You might have thought that he was a city leader of great importance. As he marched up Broadway, he looked neither to the right nor left. Today he felt himself to be a man of great responsibilities.

"I begin to feel sort of at home myself," said his wife, who always had an air of dignity. "When we was coming yesterday, New York seemed to be all strange. And there wasn't nobody expecting us. Now I feel just as if I'd been here before."

Mr. and Mrs. Pinkham were now on the edge of a better-looking part of town. It was still noisy and crowded, but it was noisy with fine carriages instead of wagons. And the sidewalks were crowded with well-dressed people. The hours for shopping and visiting were beginning. Many people on the street looked admiringly at the pleased-looking couple as they went on their way. Mrs. Pinkham was embarrassed to see herself reflected over and over in the great windows.

"I wish I had seen about a new hat before we came," she complained. "People here seem to be wearing their spring things already."

"Don't you worry, Mary Ann. I don't see anybody that looks any better than you do," said Abel, with boyish pride.

Mr. Pinkham had bought the *Herald*, and also the *Sun*. Now in the very heart of New York, they found a place to rest on the Square. They sat side by side on an empty bench, looking through the papers. Each was reading over the other's shoulder. They saw that the paragraph about their visit was indeed repeated—with little additions.

The reporter for the *Sun* had made up an interview. It almost fooled Mr. Pinkham himself, but he felt that it covered him with glory. Except for the fact that the interview was imaginary, everything Mr. Pinkham said made excellent sense. He predicted that maple sugar was the great coming crop of the

Green Mountain State. The writer even suggested that there was talk of Mr. Pinkham's presence in the nationwide maple-sugar business. He hinted that much of the money on Wall Street could be involved.

"How they do hatch up these things, don't they?" said the good man. "Well, it all sounds fine, Mary Ann."

"It says here that you are a very likeable man," smiled his wife. "It says that you have filled some of the most responsible town offices. Oh—and that you are going to attend the performance at Barnum's this evening. Why, I didn't know—who have you told about that?— who was you talking to last night, Abel?"

"I never spoke of going to Barnum's to any living soul," insisted Abel. "I only thought that I might go and take you. Now that *is* strange. Perhaps they put it in just to advertise the show."

"Ain't it kind of a low place for folks like us to be seen?" asked Mrs. Pinkham timidly. "Now that people are paying us all this attention, I don't know if it would be dignified for us to go to one of them circus places."

"I don't care. We don't live but once. I ain't coming to New York and confine myself," answered Abel. "I tell you we can spend our sugar-money any way we want to. You've worked hard and looked forward to this trip for a long time. So have I. I ain't going to mince my steps and pinch pennies for nobody. I'm going to hire one of them cabs and ride up to the Park."

"Joe Fitch said we could ride in one of those elevated railroads for five cents," protested Mary Ann. She was less eager to spend money than her husband was. But Mr. Pinkham was not to be stopped. Soon they found themselves going up Fifth Avenue in an open carriage. The spring sun shone upon them. A soft breeze fluttered the feathers on Mrs. Pinkham's plain winter hat and brought a pretty color to her cheeks.

"There! This is more like it!" Mr. Pinkham cried. "Such people as we are can't act like cheapskates. It ain't expected. Don't it make up for a lot of hard work?" His wife gave him a pleased look for her answer. They were both thinking of their gray farmhouse perched on its high hill. They thought of their old red barn, the pasture, and the shaggy woods that stretched far up the side of the mountain.

"I wish Sarah and little Abel was here to see us ride by," said Mary Ann. "I can't seem to wait for them to get that newspaper! I'm so glad we sent it right off before we started this morning. If Abel goes to the post office after school, as he always does, they'll have it to read tomorrow before supper."

III

This happy day in two plain lives ended with the great Barnum show. The next morning, Mr. and Mrs. Pinkham found themselves showered with all sorts of ads and brochures. These all added somewhat to their sense of responsibility.

Mrs. Pinkham became afraid that the hotel would charge them double.

"I don't know that I'd half mind," said the good soul. "I never did have such a splendid time in all my life, Abel. Finding you so respected way off here is the best of anything. And then seeing them dear little babies in their nice carriages up in Central Park. I never will forget them beautiful little creatures. And then the houses, and the horses, and the store windows—and all the rest of it! Well, I can't make any country pitcher hold no more! I want to get home now. Then I can think it all over while I go about my housework."

They were entering the hotel for the last time when a young man met them and bowed politely. He was the reporter who had found them on their arrival, but they did not know it. Once, that reporter had been a country boy himself. Now he wanted to see with his own eyes what effect a day of fame had had on their lives. He knew that the best fun of all would be to send copies of the story to the weekly newspapers in that part of Vermont. Now, face to face, he saw the evidence of the Pinkhams' happy increase of self-respect. He had made their whole neighborhood pay them honor. Such is the power of the press.

After the reporter had meekly passed, Mrs. Pinkham looked at her husband. "Who was that young man?—he kind of bowed to you," she asked. But Abel Pinkham, Esquire, could only tell her that he didn't know. Perhaps he was the young fellow who was sitting in the smoking-room one evening. But what did it matter? To these distinguished persons, the reporter did not seem to be a young man of any importance.

Thinking About
the Stories

A White Heron

1. Which character in this story do you most admire? Why? Which character do you like the least?

2. Many stories are meant to teach a lesson of some kind. Is the author trying to make a point in this story? What is it?

3. The plot is the series of events that takes place in a story. Usually, story events are linked in some way. Can you name an event in this story that was the cause of a later event?

The Hiltons' Holiday

1. What is the title of this story? Can you think of another good title?

2. Suppose that this story was the first chapter in a book of many chapters. What would happen next?

3. Look back at the illustration that introduces this story. What character or

characters are pictured? What is happening in the scene? What clues does the picture give you about the time and place of the story?

Fame's Little Day

1. In what town, city, or country does this story take place? Is the location important to the story? Why or why not?

2. Good writing always has an effect on the reader. How did you feel when you finished reading this story? Were you surprised, horrified, amused, sad, touched, or inspired? What elements in the story made you feel that way?

3. Who is the main character in this story? Who are one or two of the minor characters? Describe each of these characters in one or two sentences.

BLACKTOP

JUSTIN

To Mom, for dropping me off at the library

on the way to work—LA

GROSSET & DUNLAP
Penguin Young Readers Group
An Imprint of Penguin Random House LLC

Text copyright © 2016 by Penguin Random House LLC. Cover illustration copyright
© 2016 by Raul Allen. All rights reserved. Published by Grosset & Dunlap,
an imprint of Penguin Random House LLC, 345 Hudson Street, New York, New York
10014. GROSSET & DUNLAP is a trademark of Penguin Random House LLC.
Printed in the USA.

Library of Congress Cataloging-in-Publication Data is available.

ISBN 978-1-101-99562-4 (paperback)   10 9 8 7 6 5 4 3 2 1
ISBN 978-0-399-54275-6 (library binding)   10 9 8 7 6 5 4 3 2 1